J
294.
6
Aro

Arora, R. T.
Sikhism

DATE DUE

Rec 1/22/88

GARDINER LIBRARY
Gardiner, N. Y. 12525

D1307147

SIKHISM

Ranjit Arora

The Bookwright Press
New York · 1987

Religions of the World

Buddhism
Christianity
Hinduism
Islam
Judaism
Sikhism

To
my Mother and Father
and
to my sister, Surinder

MS RANJIT KAUR ARORA was brought up as a Sikh in the State of Punjab in North India. She has taught in degree colleges in India and in primary and secondary schools in the UK. She has also made extensive contributions to the initial and in-service training of teachers. She is currently the Head of the Department of Multicultural Education at Bradford and Ilkley Community College.

Acknowledgments are due to many friends who made it possible for me to write this book but I am particularly indebted to Raminder Singh for his helpful guidance and comments, to Janice Sugden for typing the script, to Kuljit, Dan and Tom for their comments as children and to Dave Dunn for his helpful editing.

First published in the
United States in 1987 by
The Bookwright Press
387 Park Avenue South
New York, NY 10016

First published in 1986 by
Wayland (Publishers) Limited
61 Western Road, Hove
East Sussex BN3 1JD, England

© Copyright 1986 Wayland (Publishers) Limited

ISBN 0-531-18067-0
Library of Congress Catalog Card Number:
85-73670

Typeset by DP Press, Sevenoaks, England
Printed in Italy by Sagdos S.p.A., Milan

Contents

What is Sikhism?

Sikhism is as much a way of life as a religion. The word Sikh is derived from the Sanskrit word *shishya*, which means "disciple." Today there are more than ten million Sikhs in the world and most of them live in the Punjab state in northern India. Approximately 250,000 Sikhs live in Britain where they form the largest Sikh community outside India. There are another 200,000 in the US and Canada. Small Sikh communities also exist in East Africa, Singapore, Malaysia, Iran, Fiji, Australia, Thailand and Hong Kong.

Sikhs believe in one God; rituals and idol worship are not part of their religion. On the whole, they are deeply religious people. This does not mean that all Sikhs follow all the teachings of the ten Sikh Gurus (religious leaders and teachers). The essence of Sikhism is that people should earn their living

The Mool Mantra was the first hymn written by Guru Nanak.

ੴ

IK ONKAAR

There is only one God

ਸਤਿਨਾਮੁ

SAT NAAM

Truth is his name

ਕਰਤਾ ਪੁਰਖ

KARTA PURKH

He is the creator

ਨਿਰਭਉ

NIRBHAU

He is without fear

ਨਿਰਵੈਰੁ

NIRVAIR

He is without hate

ਅਕਾਲ ਮੂਰਤਿ

AKAAL MOORAT

He is timeless and without form

ਅਜੂਨੀ ਸੈਭ

AJOONI SABHANG

He is beyond death — the enlightened one

ਗੁਰ ਪ੍ਰਸਾਦਿ ॥

GUR PARSAD

He can be known by the guru's grace

by honest means and hard work. It also teaches that people should share what they earn with the poor. The reason behind such thinking is that you can only love and serve God if you love and serve all the people created by God.

The Sikhs place great stress on the

In the Gurdwara, *everyone is welcome.*

equality of all human beings. Their *Gurdwaras* (places of worship) are open to everyone and all are welcome to eat in the *Langar* (community kitchen and the meal prepared there).

5

Like other world religions Sikhism has a scripture, called the *Guru Granth Sahib*, an initiation ceremony, places of pilgrimage and a distinct way of performing marriages and funerals. Sikhs can worship at any time and anywhere they happen to be, by repeating aloud, or to themselves, the hymns of the *Guru Granth Sahib*. Sikhs can be initiated, or baptized, at any age as long as they can understand and practice the teachings of the Gurus. *Granthis*, or priests, do not need any

Services in the Gurdwara *are conducted by people called* Granthis.

special training; they are ordinary people who know the Sikh scriptures and can therefore conduct a service in a *Gurdwara*.

In many ways Sikhism has become as established as many other religions. Unlike Christianity, it does not have a missionary tradition. However, voluntary converts to Sikhism are always welcomed.

The History of Sikhism

The Sikh religion is the youngest of the major world religions. It was founded by Guru Nanak in 1469 and developed to its present form over the following 200 years. The unique story of its development includes ten successive Gurus and an eventful history. Many times the Moghul emperors tried to destroy the Sikhs but were unsuccessful.

Ten Gurus

Sikhism was born in the Punjab at a time of great intolerance. Guru Nanak, the first Guru, was born into a Hindu family but was influenced by Islam as well. He joined the "Sufis" who were an Islamic mystical sect. The study of the two religions showed Guru Nanak that they had much in common. He also understood the deep conflict between

Guru Nanak, the founder of Sikhism.

them. He wanted to abolish the Hindu caste system that was responsible for so much division in Indian society. He believed that God can be found everywhere and in everyone. In an age when women were considered inferior, Guru Nanak gave women equal status with men and preached equality between all castes and creeds.

As a practical example of his teachings he took as his companions an aged Muslim musician, called Mardana, and a Hindu peasant, called Bala. The three went preaching from

An old picture showing the ten Gurus *and two followers.*

one village to another. Guru Nanak's teachings were mainly about the oneness of God and the equality of human beings.

The four Gurus that followed were all peaceful men. But when the fifth Guru and later the ninth Guru were put to death by the Moghul emperors, the Sikhs began to develop a strong sense of self-preservation. It was the tenth and last Guru, Guru Gobind Singh, who eventually organized the Sikhs into a strong militant group. He also decided that after him there would be no more Gurus, and that Sikhs should follow the teachings of the *Guru Granth Sahib*, which includes poems

Above   This painting shows a scene from the life of Guru Nanak.

The tenth and last Guru, Guru Gobind Singh, organized the Sikhs into a strong, militant group.

and hymns composed by the Gurus and by a number of other poets of different religions and castes. He also gave the Sikhs their present marks of identification (see page 21). He did not leave his followers a kingdom but laid the foundations of a community. His teachings have withstood time and are still relevant today. He was a friend to all, a fearless statesman, an excellent warrior and a great author and scholar. He wrote in Punjabi, Hindi, Persian and Sanskrit.

The Palki, *the throne of the* Guru Granth Sahib.

The creation of the *Khalsa*

The story of how the *Khalsa* was created is famous in Sikh history. Guru Gobind Singh summoned all the Sikhs to assemble on *Baisakhi* day in 1699. In uniform and fully armed, the Guru stood before his people and reminded them of the need to unite and strengthen themselves as a group. He then unsheathed his sword and made a dramatic demand in these words: "Is there anyone in this *Sangat* who is willing to offer his head for his Guru and his religion?"

Everyone was silent with fear. The Guru repeated his demand three times and the crowd became more and more afraid. Then one man, a Hindu from Lahore, came forward and offered his head. Guru Gobind Singh took him into a tent nearby and reappeared with his sword dripping in blood and repeated his demand. This time a peasant from Delhi came forward. The Guru took him into the tent and came out again demanding another head. This demand was repeated twice more and on each occasion the Guru came out of the tent with a bloodied sword. After the fifth man had entered the tent the Guru reappeared with the five men all dressed in saffron uniforms like the Guru himself, and carrying swords. Thus chosen, the "immortal five" were called *Panj Pyares* (five beloved ones) by the Guru:

My brothers, I have made you the same as I am. There is no difference between you and me. You have passed my toughest test with honor. You are my five beloved ones.

He told the shocked but relieved audience that these five were the first five members of the new brotherhood, called the *Khalsa*, or the pure ones. Members of this brotherhood must be fearless and ready to give their lives for their faith. They should also be free from restrictions of caste and therefore should first drink *Amrit* from the same bowl and then share the same surname, *Singh*, which means lion, for men, and *Kaur*, which means princess, for women.

British rule

The most popular hero of Sikh history is a man who became Maharajah of a large Sikh state. Ranjit Singh (1780–1839) was known as the "Lion of the Punjab." During his lifetime, the British were taking over most of India.

Ranjit Singh's death in 1839 was virtually the death of the Sikh kingdom. The British had for a long time been frustrated by the strength of the Sikh Army. In 1849, the Punjab became part of British India. The best part of the Sikh Army was incorporated into the British Army. The Sikh soldiers were allowed to wear turbans and to keep long hair and beards as prescribed by their religion.

In 1857, when most parts of India revolted against the British, the Sikhs in the Punjab remained loyal. For the first fifty years of British rule the Sikhs were content. Things began to change when land became scarce and growing Sikh families could no longer provide for themselves. The younger men emigrated to other states in India and to countries outside India. Contact with the outside world made the Sikhs more aware of their political rights in

During World War I, many Sikhs fought as part of the British Army.

Right   *A batallion of the Sikh Infantry, part of today's modern Indian Army.*

their own country. The *Singh Sabha*, established in 1870, increased their strength through education and literature. Sikh schools were opened in different parts of the Punjab.

Some of the bullet holes made during the Jallianwala Bagh massacre in 1919.

festival of *Baisakhi* because they were afraid that the Sikhs would revolt against them. However, the Sikhs did assemble at a place called Jallianwala Bagh in Amritsar. The army was instructed by an officer to open fire and more than 1,500 people were killed.

The Sikh *Gurdwaras* Act of 1925 appointed a committee which was responsible to the Indian Government for Sikh affairs in the Punjab. This committee was put in charge of all Sikh *Gurdwaras* and shrines. British rule came to an end in 1947.

The division of India

India was divided in 1947 and part of it became Pakistan. The new country of Pakistan, under Muslim leadership, included part of the Punjab. The Sikhs did not want the Punjab to be divided but they had no choice but to accept the partition. Nearly two and a half million Sikhs had to leave their homes, lands and *Gurdwaras* and move to India as refugees.

As a result the Sikhs tried to establish a Sikh state, *Punjabi Suba*, and fought for their fair share in education, employment, industry and politics. It was not until 1966 that they succeeded in gaining recognition and a Punjabi-speaking state came into being. Today, the Punjab is still part of India, though many Sikhs continue to strive for their own independent homeland.

During World War I (1914–18) the Sikhs fought in the British Army. But in 1918 they clashed with the British over who should control the *Gurdwaras* and shrines. In 1919, the British had forbidden Sikhs to gather for the

Places of Worship

The most important communal aspect of Sikh prayer and worship is when it is held in congregational form in a *Gurdwara*. The word literally means the "House of God." Wherever the Sikhs are settled as a community they establish a *Gurdwara*. Most of them are in existing buildings which have been converted to suit the needs of the Sikh community — outside India only a small number have been especially built as *Gurdwaras*. Sometimes Sikhs use a hired public hall or a member's house as a *Gurdwara*.

Inside the *Gurdwara*, the *Guru Granth Sahib* is treated with great respect. It is covered with richly embroidered cloths and it rests on cushions in a specially made *Palki*, a throne which looks a bit like a small four-poster bed. Before entering the building, Sikhs take off their shoes and cover their heads. They

Offerings of money are made by Sikhs when they visit their Gurdwara.

approach the *Guru Granth Sahib*, bow before it in reverence and place their offerings, usually money, say their prayers, back away respectfully and find a place to sit on the floor. Men usually sit on one side and women on the other. This segregation is a cultural tradition developed over the years.

Some families keep a copy of the *Guru Granth Sahib* in a special room at home where they can go for prayer and meditation, or have small gatherings of their friends on ceremonial occasions.

The service in *Gurdwaras* is usually

Men usually sit on one side of the Gurdwara *and women on the other.*

conducted in Punjabi, the language of the Punjab. Sikh children who have not been born and raised in India, often find it difficult to understand this complex language. For their benefit some common hymns and prayers have been translated into English and sometimes part of the service is also conducted in English. This also helps those visitors to *Gurdwaras* who do not speak Punjabi.

Generally, Sikhs regard any day as a holy day. *Gurdwaras* are therefore open to everyone throughout the week. But the Christian tradition of Sunday worship has had an influence, and many Sikhs go to the *Gurdwara* on Sunday.

The service lasts from three to four hours but people are free to come and go as they please. The atmosphere is pleasant and informal. The service consists of short readings from the *Guru Granth Sahib*, explanations of the scriptures, and hymn singing by musicians. It is concluded by a common prayer. Then *Karah Parsad* is distributed. Finally, *Langar*, (a meal prepared in the community kitchen), is served to all visitors free of charge. Since everyone (Sikh or non-Sikh) is

At the end of a Sikh service, Karah Parsad *is given to all present.*

After the service everyone shares a meal called Langar.

welcome to the *Gurdwara*, and no one has to pay for the meal, the practice of *Langar* is very much in line with what the Sikh Gurus wanted — for people to meet and break bread together regardless of caste and class distinctions thereby encouraging social equality. *Gurdwaras* are also used as Sunday schools for teaching Punjabi. Weddings and festivals are celebrated there and it is also used as a community center for informal social meetings.

The Golden Temple

The Golden Temple, also known as "The Temple of God," is one of the many *Gurdwaras* in India which were built by a Guru and is very special to Sikhs. It is in the city of Amritsar (which means "Tank of Nectar") in the Punjab. It is regarded as a place of pilgrimage by Sikhs throughout the world.

The foundation of the Golden Temple was laid by a Muslim follower of the fifth Guru. The Guru built four doors, one on each side, to emphasize that the Sikh place of worship is open to people from all four castes and from all four corners of the earth.

It is this temple that has been in the news during the conflicts in recent years between Sikhs and the Government of India. The Sikhs were angry when the temple was attacked and partly demolished by the Indian Army in 1984.

The architecture of the Golden Temple is a mixture of Hindu and Muslim artistic traditions. It is a two-story marble structure and is built on a 20 m (67 ft) square platform in the center of the sacred pool. The central dome of the temple and the upper half of the walls are covered with gold-

plated copper sheets, hence the name Golden Temple. There is also a small hall of mirrors (*Shish Mahal*) on the upper story.

All visitors are welcome but they have to take off their shoes and cover their heads to come inside. There are a

The Golden Temple at Amritsar is a place of pilgrimage for Sikhs.

number of other interesting buildings around the Golden Temple. There is also a Sikh museum containing articles of religious and literary importance.

Basic Beliefs

The basic beliefs of Sikhism make it a religion of modern times. It believes in a society where men and women are equal and democracy is practiced in everyday life. Guru Nanak's main teachings were based on the principle that "there is no Hindu, there is no Muslim, but only one human being who is a disciple of God." He also preached the oneness of God, a God without physical qualities or images but present in all people and all things.

The way of practicing religion as shown by the ten Sikh Gurus is not based on rigid rules or laws but on the teachings of the ten Gurus, as set out in the *Guru Granth Sahib*, which now serve as the guiding force for all Sikhs, shaping their careers and their lives.

The teachings of the ten Gurus are set out in the Guru Granth Sahib, *the Sikh holy book.*

The five Ks

The five religious symbols that are usually an indication of a devout Sikh are commonly known as the five Ks. This is because they all begin with the Punjabi letter which sounds identical to "K." The five symbols are.

1. *Kesh*, which generally means hair, but in the context of Sikh religion it means uncut or long hair. Sikhs believe

A stall in Amritsar from which Sikhs can buy the Kanga *and the* Kara.

that as far as possible the course of nature should not be disturbed. The growth of hair is a natural process and therefore hair should not be cut from any part of the body.

2. *Kanga*, which means a small wooden comb. This is usually required to keep long hair well groomed.

A Sikh boy proudly shows his Kirpan.

3. *Kara*, which is a steel bangle worn on the right wrist by men, women and children. The steel represent strength and its round shape the unending circle of continuity.

4. *Kirpan*, which is a small sword and is a symbol of self-defense and the fight against evil and injustice.

5. *Kachha*, which means a pair of shorts made to a specific design. These formed part of the military uniform in Guru Gobind Singh's day and are also a symbol of sexual restraint.

Sikhism as a way of life

The main ideals that influence the way of life for a Sikh are based on the following beliefs:

1. Equality
All human beings are equal because God is contained in every heart. The distinctions of caste, color and creed perpetuate the inequalities that are created by selfish human beings.
2. Worship of God or *Nam*
Since the Sikhs believe God to be present everywhere, prayers can be said anywhere and at any time. However, the best times for prayers are considered to be before dawn, early evening, or dusk, and last thing at night. At these times Sikhs believe it is easier to concentrate and establish communion with God.
3. Dignity of Labor
Dignity of labor is described in Punjabi as *Kirat Karni*, which means earning one's living by honest means and working hard for one's livelihood. Sikhism condemns idleness or a tendency to live off others. Gainful employment is important to build up the self-confidence and dignity of individuals. For Sikhs there is dignity of labor in any job provided it is legal and ethical. Use of dishonest means to accumulate wealth is regarded as a sin.
4. Giving of Charity
Living and sharing is shown in the concern for the needs of the poor, and

deprived sections of the human race. Guru Nanak said, "Having earned wages as a due reward of honest labor, we must dutifully share the surplus with others." One way of achieving this as practiced by true Sikhs is the

Most Sikhs have long hair. This is called Kesh *and is one of the Sikh religious symbols known as the five Ks.*

donation of ten percent of one's income for the benefit of society.

Preparing for Langar, *as part of the* Sewa *or service*.

5. Service or *Sewa*

Sewa, the performance of selfless service, is understood in two senses; first there is the service to God. This may be performed in the following ways — reading aloud from the scriptures; contributing to the upkeep of a *Gurdwara*; helping with its repairs and daily cleaning; sharing in the cooking and serving of *Langar*.

The second sense is service to other human beings. This usually takes the form of hospitality offered by the Sikhs both in their homes and in *Gurdwaras* where meals are served free of charge to anyone irrespective of color, caste or creed.

Life and death

Sikhs believe that they live many lives, but only when they are born into a human body can they fully worship the God who created them. They believe that they have lived before as an animal, a plant or even as a stone. When they die, Sikhs believe they will be reborn in some other form. Therefore, death should not cause sadness to those left behind.

At Sikh funerals, families say goodbye to their dead relative. The prayer said by Sikhs before they go to sleep is also used at funerals, symbolizing that death is similar to sleep and should not be mourned. Afterward the body is cremated and the ashes scattered in running water.

The Sikh Code of Conduct

Most features of the Sikh code of conduct were introduced by the tenth Guru, and they are still very relevant in today's world. For instance:

1. Sikhs are forbidden to remove hair from the head, face or other part of their body. Sanctity of *Kesh* (hair) must be maintained at all times.

2. Sikhs are forbidden to commit adultery. The relationship between two people within marriage must be respected.

3. Sikhs are forbidden to smoke or chew tobacco or related substances.

Intoxicants of any kind are seen as harmful to the human mind.

4. Sikhs are forbidden to eat meat from ritually killed animals, i.e. Halal or Kosher. Halal meat (from animals killed according to Muslim rituals) is fobidden as the ritual is said to cause prolonged suffering to the animal. Many Sikhs do not eat beef because of the Hindu influence. (Hindus regard the cow as a sacred animal.)

Sikh dress

Sikh men are expected to wear the turban, which clearly indicates their religion. Turbans are also exchanged

This Sikh wears the turban, which identifies his religion.

as a sign of friendship on festive occasions. In India Sikh boys do not usually wear a turban until they reach maturity, but in other countries boys often begin to wear a turban when they start school. Sikh women dress modestly but can wear whatever they like.

Sikh names

Soon after the birth of a child the parents visit the *Gurdwara* to pray and to decide on a name for their child. This is done by opening the *Guru Granth Sahib* at random and the first letter of the hymn on the left hand page is taken as the first letter of a child's personal name. The second name for a boy is usually *Singh* and for a girl it is *Kaur*. Since Sikhism rejects the use of caste or subcaste names, "Singh" and "Kaur" are sometimes used as surnames.

A Sikh family prays in a place of pilgrimage in India. They are choosing a name for their baby.

Amrit ceremony (baptism)

The *Amrit* ceremony is similar to the Christian confirmation. It is intended to bring Sikhs into full membership in their faith. They should only take *Amrit* when they are mature enough to realize the obligations that this demands. *Amrit* is a drink prepared by stirring water and crystallized sugar in a steel bowl with a double-edged sword. During its preparation, five hymns from the *Guru Granth Sahib* are recited.

Marriage

Sikhs regard marriage as a sacred bond of mutual dependence between a man and a woman. Ideally, the wife and husband are united in spirit as well as in mind and body. Marriage is also regarded as an equally strong bond between the other members of both families and the bride and groom.

A Sikh woman drinks sugar and water as part of the Amrit *ceremony.*

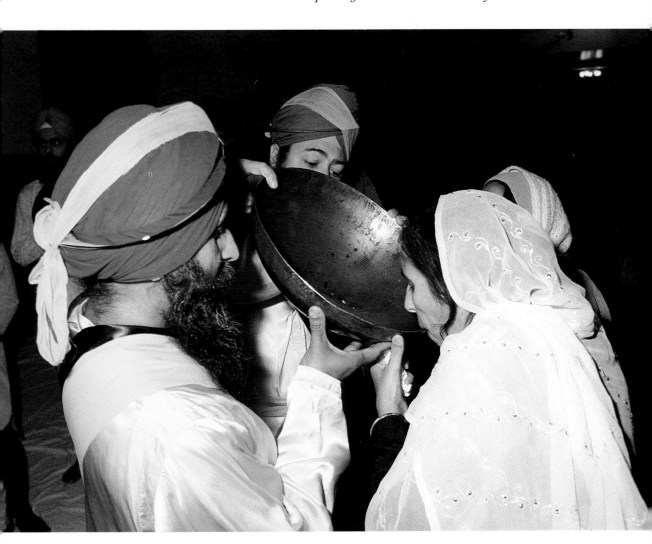

During a Sikh wedding the bride and groom receive gifts of money.

The actual wedding ceremony take place in the presence of the *Guru Grantn Sahib*. In fact that is the only witnes necessary for a Sikh marriage. The couple sit in front of the *Guru Grantn Sahib* with their parents close by. The *Granthi* performs the ceremony with special wedding hymns and a prayer With each verse the couple slowly wall around the *Guru Granth Sahib*, and during the last circuit friends and relatives throw rose petals at the couple.

After the reception the bride leaves with the groom and his parents for her new home. This is usually a very sac and emotional time for the bride and her parents. It signifies the fina departure of their daughter who has now become a wife and has a new family to which she belongs.

Family life

Sikh families, like most Indian families, have a tradition of extended or joint family. This means that a family unit includes grandparents and sometimes a number of married and unmarried uncles, aunts and cousins. Today, however, most Sikh families are divided, with some members living in India, their country of origin, and others living abroad. Some also choose to live as a smaller nuclear family, that is, both parents, their children, and possibly one or more grandparent. For Sikhs who live outside India, this is not

The choice of partners is very carefully made to avoid big differences in the standard of living and level of education of the partners. Sikh marriages are not initially based on mutual love between a girl and a boy but more on the potential of creating a happy and loving home together.

always a matter of choice because houses abroad are usually not large enough for extended families.

Whatever the size of the family, a Sikh home provides a happy and secure atmosphere for children. There is a great deal of love and affection between brothers and sisters. The relationship beween husband and wife is of secondary importance. The most important thing is for sons and daughters to care for their parents.

The family is the basic unit in the Sikh community.

Sikhs maintain this strong and supportive family structure in many different ways. Weekly visits to the *Gurdwara* are usually family occasions as are weddings, engagements, funerals and parties to celebrate birthdays. Traveling long distances to visit friends and relatives is also a common family activity.

29

Sikh Women

In some ways, the Sikh Gurus were more successful in achieving sexual equality in the fifteenth century than has been possible for women generally in the twentieth century. They not only raised their voices against the customs of *purdah* and *suttee*, but also gave women equal rights to participate in religious services. Sikh women can become *Granthis*, perform *Kirtan*, solemnize marriages and be one of the "five beloved ones" at the *Amrit* ceremony. The following extract from the *Guru Granth Sahib* shows the strength of the Sikh Gurus' feelings on the subject.

> It is by women we are conceived and from them that we are born. It is with them that we are betrothed and married. It is the women we befriend and it is the women who keep the race going. When one woman dies we seek another. It is with women that we become established in society. Why should women be called inferior when they give birth to great men?

Women in a Gurdwara *are on equal terms with men.*

Women in Sikh families play a very central and important role. They may appear extremely modest and withdrawn in mixed company but they fully participate within the family and the community. Sikh women have played a positive role in every chapter of Sikh history. It was their fight

Sikh women play an important role as individuals in the Gurdwara. They often lead the congregation in prayer.

against the oppression of the Moghul rulers, side by side with their menfolk, that has helped to make the Sikh community what it is today.

them have jobs outside the home. Removal of *purdah* gave Sikh women the strength and confidence to become self-respecting individuals.

Although in a religious sense Sikh women are considered equal to men and are given an honored place in the community, social and cultural conventions make it difficult for them to benefit equally from opportunities in education and employment. Sikh families treat girls less favorably than boys, and girls do not enjoy the same degree of freedom as their brothers. The Sikh code of conduct was intended equally for men and women but in practice there are different expect-ations for men and women. These are largely imposed by cultural traditions.

Girls in many Sikh families are considered to be a big responsibility. The majority of Sikh parents still expect their daughters to get married at an early age and have children. Although they are allowed to benefit from educational opportunities, the ultimate goal for their lives is still to be a wife and a mother rather than to pursue careers. In spite of the relatively liberal attitude toward women, Sikh parents still find it difficult to break social and cultural conventions and to treat a daughter in the same way as a son. For example, the prospect of a daughter living away from home to pursue further education or a career is far more daunting to parents than the prospect of a son's doing the same.

Some Sikh families still expect their daughters to marry and have children rather than to pursue careers.

Sikh women of today are responsible, independent people. They play a leading role in the services and organization of *Gurdwaras* and most of

The Sikh Community

The Sikhs who have made a home away from India are rapidly adapting to the ways of life of their adopted countries. Like any other migrant group they have had to make many changes in their religious, social and cultural beliefs. For example, when some Sikhs could not get jobs because they wore the turban, they decided to stop wearing it. But this did not stop them from being Sikhs or from leading good lives as Sikhs.

Most Sikh parents do not object to having their children learn about other

London, England, the site of this busy street scene, is home for many Sikhs.

A music teacher (left) and his pupils.

religions in school, but they do provide some instruction in their own religion at home. The *Gurdwaras* are another source of information about religion but there is very little attempt there to teach religion to Sikh children. The Sunday schools are mainly for teaching the Punjabi language.

Although Sikhism rejects distinctions on the basis of caste and class, in practice there are some social groups based on caste distinctions. These are obvious only to people who are part of these groups. Free social mixing of such groups is quite common. The only visible effect of such distinctions is in the arrangement of marriages between members of different caste groups.

Sikhs generally place great value on hard work, and individual achievement. They are eager to take on any opportunity in education, employment or business. This is why they can be found at all levels of commercial, industrial and professional sectors wherever they live. The close-knit Sikh community provides support for individuals. It also reinforces the need to maintain links with life in the Punjab and to preserve the Punjabi culture and Sikh identity.

Until recently, *Gurdwaras* have been the only meeting place for Sikh social and cultural events. But the leaders in *Gurdwaras* have been more concerned with the religious affairs of the community. Over recent years, Sikh youth has organized itself as a group with different views from those of the older generation. Young Sikhs find that some of the traditional values of their parents are different from the values of the modern society in which they live. They are also more conscious of their position in such a society and are prepared to stand up for their rights. The open and secure family atmosphere encourages them to express their feelings with confidence.

For both parents and children, Sikh community groups are a source of advice and strength. They are also used as a link with public institutions such as schools and colleges.

As a community, Sikhs are likely to

Sikhs keep their traditions of music and dancing alive wherever they go.

preserve their distinctive identity. The religious identity of second generation Sikhs — those who were born and brought up away from India — may have a different public image but the basic beliefs and code of conduct are still as relevant as they were 500 years ago. Second generation Sikhs are also creating a new Punjabi culture, but the Punjabi folk culture is still intact and is developing through music, dance and literature.

Sikhs have close religious and cultural links with Hindus. Guru Tegh Bahadur, the ninth Guru, sacrificed his life to protect the Hindus of Kashmir from Muslim rulers. Like other Sikh Gurus, Guru Tegh Bahadur was as much against the idol worship practiced by Hindus as the Muslim

rulers were. Defending an ideology in which he himself did not believe appears to be contradictory. But, in fact, he was defending their right to practice their religion. He was also defending Hindus from the Muslim rulers who were forcing them to become Muslim. In a sense he was putting into practice Guru Nanak's teaching which says:

If a strong power attacks another strong power
No one would grieve, none would complain
But when fierce tigers prey on helpless cattle
Then herdsmen must answer for it.

The recent tensions between Hindus and Sikhs are caused by the Sikhs' fear of being absorbed into the predominantly Hindu Indian community and losing their separate indentity.

A community gathering laying the foundations of a London Gurdwara.

Language and Culture

The development of Punjabi

The growth of the Punjabi language has increased even though the size of the Punjab has shrunk. Punjabi is one of the many regional languages of India. It is spoken by more than 20 million Hindus, Sikhs and Muslims in India and Pakistan. Since 1966, Punjabi has also become the official language of the Indian state of Punjab. This state is the homeland of Sikhs. The written form of Punjabi spoken in the Punjab is in *Gurmukhi* script. This

The written form of Punjabi is called Gurmukhi *script. It is written from left to right.*

script was used by the second Guru to write down the hymns composed by Guru Nanak.

As a spoken language, Punjabi is similar to Hindi and Urdu. In its written form it has some Hindi influence in the shape of its letters. Like Hindi, Punjabi is written from left to right.

Punjabi literature has a rich tradition of poets and writers of different faiths. Punjabi poetry written by famous Muslim poets forms part of popular Punjabi literature. However, this was originally written in Persian script.

Today's Punjabi literature includes a wide range of novels, short stories, plays and poetry. Some of it has also been translated into other languages.

The Punjabi language of everyday

ਦੇਹ ਸ਼ਿਵਾ ਬਰ ਮੋਹਿ ਇਹੈ ਸ਼ੁਭ ਕਰਮਨ ਤੇ ਕਬਹੂੰ ਨ ਟਰੋਂ
ਨ ਡਰੋਂ ਅਰਿ ਸੋ ਜਬ ਜਾਇ ਲਰੋਂ ਨਿਸਚੈ ਕਰ ਅਪਨੀ ਜੀਤ ਕਰੋਂ
ਅਰੁ ਸਿਖ ਹੋਂ ਆਪਨੇ ਹੀ ਮਨ ਕੋ ਇਹ ਲਾਲਚ ਹਉ ਗੁਨ ਤਉ ਉਚਰੋਂ
ਜਬ ਆਵ ਕੀ ਅਉਧ ਨਿਧਾਨ ਬਨੈ ਅਤ ਹੀ ਰਨ ਮੈ ਤਬ ਜੂਝ ਮਰੋਂ

use has a rich vocabulary, but is simple and extremely polite and gentle. The language of the scriptures is difficult because it has a rich heritage of Persian, Sanskrit and Hindi. It is therefore very different from spoken, everyday Punjabi in the same way that everyday English is very different from the language of the Bible.

Culture

Punjabi culture is a rich combination of folklore and popular traditions of art and craft. The language used for its

A colorful group of folk dancers from the Punjab performing Bhangra.

expression is also very colorful.

Punjabi folk songs and dances are shared by all the people living in the Punjab and are not associated with religion. *Bhangra* is the most famous folk dance of the Punjab. It is usually associated with harvest time in India. The female counterpart of *Bhangra* is *Giddha*, a folk dance performed only by women.

Sikhs believe that music is good for

Musicians in a Gurdwara *accompany the singing of* Kirtan.

the soul. It is an important part of the Sikh faith. Devotional music known as *Kirtan* includes the singing of hymns accompanied by harmonium and tabla (a pair of small drums) as well as other instruments. The scriptures also are composed and sung in the true tradition of Indian classical music.

Festivals

Generally, Sikhs participate in a number of Indian festivals, such as *Baisakhi*, *Diwali* and *Holi* (which has become the Sikh *Hola Mohalla*) which are not always associated with the Sikh religion. There are also a number of holy festivals known as *Gurpurbs* that are celebrated only by Sikhs. These include the birthdays of Guru Nanak

An elephant is dressed for the Guru Tegh Bahadur festival.

and Guru Gobind Singh, the martyrdom days of Guru Arjun Dev and Guru Tegh Bahadur, the anniversary of the death of Maharajah Ranjit Singh.

The dates for these festivals vary because they are dependent on a lunar calendar that is based on the movements of the moon. But there is one festival that falls on the same date every year. This is the festival of *Baisakhi* which always falls on April 13.

Baisakhi is the start of the Punjabi New Year, and coincides with the harvesting of crops. It is usually celebrated by all Indians with great enthusiasm. It has special significance for Sikhs because the Khalsa was created on *Baisakhi* day in 1699.

There are many other festivals, called *melas*, or "fairs." These include *Basant*, a spring festival, celebrated by Sikhs and Hindus. Most people try to wear something yellow, which is a

A date chart of Sikh festivals, which are celebrated by the lunar calendar.

Calendar months	Sikh festivals	
Magh *(Jan – Feb)*	*Maghi*	*Basant*
Phagan *(Feb – Mar)*	*Hola Mohalla*	
Chait *(Mar – Apr)*		
Vasakh *(Apr – May)*	*Baisakhi* (April 13)	
Jaith *(May – Jun)*	The martyrdom of Guru Arjan	
Har *(Jun – July)*	Birthday of Guru Har Krishan	
Sawan *(July – Aug)*		
Bhadro *(Aug – Sept)*	*Rakhsha Bandhan*	
Asun *(Sept – Oct)*	Installation of the Guru Granth Sahib	Birthday of Guru Ram Das
Katik *(Oct – Nov)*	*Diwali*	Birthday of Guru Nanak
Magar *(Nov – Dec)*	The martyrdom of Guru Tegh Bahadur	
Poh *(Dec – Jan)*	Birthday of Guru Gobind Singh	*Lohri*

spring color, and the main meal of the day includes specially prepared yellow rice. *Basant* has come to have a meaning similar to St. Valentine's Day. It is also a special day when five-year-olds start school.

Another *mela* is *Maghi*, which is celebrated in January and honors Guru Gobind Singh who was beseiged by the Moghul Army at Anandpur in the seventeenth century. *Lohri*, also celebrated in January, marks the end of winter in India. It is also a festival for young women who pray that they will make a happy marriage.

Festival garlands for sale at a stall in Amritsar.

42

Sikhs Today

Sikhs are proud of their history and try to live up to the reputation of their religious and political leaders of the last 500 years. As a minority they have fought for the right to practice their own religion.

In 1947 when the British left India, many Sikhs had no choice but to leave their homes, lands and *Gurdwaras* in Pakistan and move to India as refugees. When the Sikh political party *Akali Dal* gained control of the Punjab the situation began to improve.

State boundaries were drawn in India according to the languages spoken in each region; each state was given a separate administrative unit. But the Punjab was left as a state without a clear ruling on language. The Sikhs agitated against this discrimination and called for *Punjabi Suba*.

Eventually, in 1966, the Indian Government did agree to form a Punjab state on the basis of language. But the actual size was much smaller than the Sikhs had expected. So the pressure for readjustment of the boundaries has continued.

These maps show the position of the Punjab, the traditional home of Sikhs.

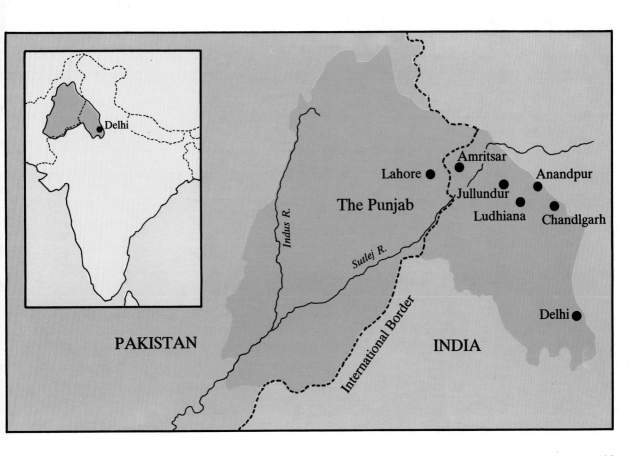

43

During the last two decades Sikhs have been mainly concerned with preserving their separate identity and with getting their equal share in the political, economic and religious spheres of the nation. But Sikhs are in a minority as they form only 2 percent of the population in India even though in the Punjab they form over 60 percent of the population.

A Sikh testing electronic components.

In other countries too, Sikhs are a minority, but all Sikhs have their origins in the state of Punjab. Faithful to their religious beliefs, Sikhs are willing to go anywhere to find work. Even people who were landowners in the Punjab have become laborers or business people in other parts of the world. Some have done very well for themselves and occupy responsible positions as magistrates, city officials, teachers, doctors and engineers.

Sikh children living in a Western country benefit from two cultures.

Wherever they live, Sikhs are regarded as members of a black community. As such, like other minority groups, they are often discriminated against in education, employment and in other areas of public service. Many Sikh men have found it impossible to get jobs unless they stop wearing turbans and get rid of their long hair. Sikh boys are laughed at by other children because they looked so different with their long hair tied up in a knot on their heads. Like children from other minority groups. Sikh children are often not able to use their own language in school. But they benefit from their knowledge of two languages and two cultures.

On the whole, Sikhs have adapted very well and have learned to cope with two different worlds. In many ways they have the best of both worlds; they are able to choose the most appropriate of the lifestyles open to them.

The way people live today is determined not only by religious beliefs but also by economic, political and social circumstances. Twentieth century Sikhism is not entirely free of caste divisions, which become more important when marriage is being considered. Some *Gurdwaras* in Britain also have a particular caste group bias because they are managed by members of that group. But all *Gurdwaras* still remain open to everyone regardless of their color, caste or creed.

Most Sikhs have a strong sense of identity. By spreading themselves to all parts of the world they have established Sikhism as a world faith.

Glossary

Amrit The Sikh baptism ceremony. It also refers to a solution of sugar crystals and water used at the initiation ceremony.

Baisakhi An Indian festival that takes its name from the Indian lunar month in which the festival falls. It takes place in April and celebrates the year's harvest. For Sikhs, it also celebrates the founding of the *Khalsa*.

Diwali The Indian Festival of Lights. It usually occurs in October or November and is celebrated throughout India.

Granthi A reader of the *Guru Granth Sahib* who can also act as a teacher and a priest.

Gurdwaras Sikh places of worship. The word *gurdwara* means "House of God."

Gurmukhi The script in which Punjabi is written.

Gurpurb The anniversary of an important event in Sikh history. It usually refers to the birth or death of a Guru.

Guru Granth Sahib The holy book of the Sikhs. It is written in Punjabi verse.

Holi The festival of color, usually celebrated in March and very popular throughout India.

Kachha A pair of shorts worn as an undergarment by Sikhs — one of the five Ks.

Kanga A small comb — one of the five Ks.

Kara A steel bangle worn on the right wrist — one of the five Ks.

Karah Parsad A sweet dough made of flour, sugar and clarified butter, which is shared out at the end of a Sikh service to everyone present.

Kesh Uncut hair — one of the five Ks.

Khalsa Brotherhood of baptized Sikhs — the word means "pure ones."

Kirpan A small sword worn by Sikhs — one of the five Ks.

Kirtan The recitation and singing of religious hymns to music.

Kirat Karni To earn one's living by one's own hard work. It is regarded as one of the basic Sikh ways of life.

Langar This word means "free kitchen." It applies to the kitchen in a *Gurdwara* and the food prepared and eaten in it.

Nam The name of God, the divine name — literally it means "name."

Panj Pyares The five beloved ones who made up the first *Khalsa*. Today the term refers to the five baptized Sikhs who perform baptisms in a *Gurdwara*.

Punjabi Suba A Punjabi-speaking state in India. It first came into being in 1966.

Purdah The practice of hiding women from the view of men or strangers; also the veil usually worn by Muslim women. This was one of the customs Sikh Gurus tried to abolish.

Sangat A congregation or a gathering of Sikhs in a *Gurdwara*.

Singh Sabha The name given to a religious association concerned with the religious and educational development of Sikhs in India.

Sewa The service given by Sikhs, both to their fellow human beings and to God. *Sewa* means "service."

Suttee A former Hindu custom whereby a widow burned herself to death on her husband's funeral pyre.

Books to Read

Aggarwal, Manju. *I Am a Sikh*. New York: Franklin Watts, 1985.

Bahree, Pat. *Hinduism*. North Pomfret, VT: David & Charles, 1984.

Berger, Gilda. *Religion*. New York: Franklin Watts, 1983.

Galbraith, Catherine A. and Rama Mehta. *India Now and Through Time*. Boston: Houghton Mifflin, 1980.

Moskin, Marietta. *In the Name of God: Religion in Everyday Life*. New York: Atheneum, 1980.

Ogle, Carol and John Ogle. *Through the Year in India*. North Pomfret, VT: David & Charles, 1983.

Seeger, Elizabeth. *Eastern Religions*. New York: Crowell Junior Books, 1973.

Singh, Daljit and Angela Smith. *The Sikh World*. Morristown, NJ: Silver Burdett, 1985.

Tames, Richard. *Islam*. North Pomfret, VT: David & Charles, 1985.

Triggs, Tony D. *Founders of Religions*. Morristown, NJ: Silver Burdett.

Picture Acknowledgments

The publisher would like to thank all those who provided the illustrations on the following pages: Camerapix *cover*, 10, 23; Colorpix 14, 19; Chris Fairclough 27; Sally & Richard Greenhill 16, 17, 22, 25, 39; The Hutchison Library 20, 23, 25, 32, 33, 35, 36, 42, 44; Imperial War Museum, London 12; Ann & Bury Peerless 7, 8, 9 (bottom), 13, 15, 21, 26, 29, 34, 40; Malcolm Walker 6, 43; Mike Walters 5, 6, 9 (top), 18, 24, 28, 30, 37, 45.

Index